M. F. (Michael Ferrebee) Sadler

The Irish Church question

a letter to the clergy of the Diocese of Ely

M. F. (Michael Ferrebee) Sadler

The Irish Church question
a letter to the clergy of the Diocese of Ely

ISBN/EAN: 9783744741255

Printed in Europe, USA, Canada, Australia, Japan

Cover: Foto ©Lupo / pixelio.de

More available books at **www.hansebooks.com**

THE

IRISH CHURCH QUESTION:

A

LETTER

TO THE

CLERGY OF THE DIOCESE OF ELY,

BY THE

REV. M. F. SADLER, M.A.,

PROCTOR IN CONVOCATION FOR THE DIOCESE,
PREBENDARY OF WELLS, AND VICAR OF ST. PAUL'S, BEDFORD.

———oo⦂⦂oo———

Bedford:
PRINTED AND PUBLISHED BY J. R. PORTER, 5, HIGH STREET.
London:
BELL AND DALDY, YORK STREET, COVENT GARDEN.

CONTENTS:

MY REVEREND BRETHREN,

Since you did me the honour of electing me a Proctor to represent you in Convocation, the question of the Irish Church has assumed proportions such as no one at that time could possibly have anticipated. I have been compelled to take upon this question a line very distasteful to the great majority of those whom I am assumed to represent.

I consequently feel bound to bring before each one of you my reasons for believing that the legislature will do a wise and just act if it terminates the existence of the Church of Ireland, as the Established Church of that part of the Empire.

The views I take upon this question I have had two opportunities of stating to my brother clergy; the first at a meeting called by the Archdeacon of Bedford, to petition in favour of the retention of the Irish Establishment; the second, on the occasion of a motion for a similar object in the Lower House of Convocation. I shall now simply repeat the substance of what I said on these occasions, adding to it such remarks of my own, or extracts from public documents and speeches in Parliament, as seem to confirm my views.

I hold, then, that the Establishment of the Anglican Church in Ireland is a just cause of offence to the people of Ireland, for it simply amounts to this, that we insist upon imposing upon them a state of things which we should resist with all our might, if any foreign power attempted to impose it upon us.

But along with this I hold that the wholesale disendowment of the Irish Church, as it is proposed by some of the leaders of the Liberal party, would be a grievous wrong to a section of the people of Ireland, on whom this country has relied for upwards of three centuries for keeping its hold upon the island, and without whose aid it assuredly would not now be a part of the Queen's dominions.

Before attempting to show my reasons for holding these two propositions, let me answer an objection which meets me at the outset, which is that I cannot hold these two opinions together. I am told that dis-establishment and dis-endowment must of necessity go together ; that it is impossible to separate them. Some people, sensible enough in other matters, profess to be unable to see any distinction between them.

I own I am astounded at such a confusion of two things so utterly apart, seeing that we see these two things existing all around us in perfect separation from one another. We see on all sides establishment without endowment, and endowment without establishment.

We have establishment without endowment. We have a large and an increasing number of churches built without any aid whatsoever from the State, and depending both for the stipend of the minister and for the carrying on of Divine service, not on tithes or endowments of any sort, not even on pew rents, but on the weekly offertory. Moreover, in some of these churches the magnificence of ritual (all involving heavy expense) is such as (in the view of many amongst us) loudly to call for legislative interference in the way of restraint. The musical part of the services in some of these churches costs, I am told, £800 or £1000 a year. The offertories altogether amount to £1000, £1200, £1400, and in one or two cases, £1800 a year.

These churches, so far as maintenance is concerned, are the most purely "voluntary" that can be conceived, and yet they all are "established," because by the act of consecration they are brought under the superintendence of a bishop, who happens to be an officer of an establishment.

Then, conversely, we have on all sides Endowment without Establishment. We have throughout the country a large number of Dissenting meeting houses, (far more than most persons have any idea of) which are more or less endowed. There are two such meeting houses in the parish of which I am the incumbent; so that there is no necessary connection whatsoever between establishment and endowment.

But still though the things are so distinct it is argued that in the present case they must go together.

Now I shall proceed to shew that a very considerable number of the leading speakers in the recent parliamentary debates on the Irish Church question, and especially on the so called Liberal side, carefully distinguish between these two things.

First of all, the Right Hon. Robert Lowe, in his speech on Mr. Gladstone's Resolutions, on Thursday, April 2nd, expressed himself thus:—

"The Church of the twelve per cent is not only endowed, but it is established. The Queen is its head, its Bishops sit by rotation in the House of Lords, it has ecclesiastical courts, established and maintained at the public expense to decide ecclesiastical questions arising among this small body; and the whole establishment is so constituted as if to point and give a sting to the inequality which exists."

On the same evening Mr. Bernal Osborne expressed himself thus:—

"Now, sir, there are two distinct questions involved in these resolutions. First, the question of dis-establishment, and next, the question of dis-endowment. I state that these are totally distinct questions. It has been remarked by a writer on the subject, that men are so apt to confound their spiritual convictions with their personal interests, that an attack upon the property of the Church is always more apt to cause irritation than an attack upon its doctrines. Now shall I decline altogether to discuss the question as a mere money question. My opinion is that money is quite a secondary element in it, &c."

In the same debate we have Lord Stanley (a statesman, all whose sympathies are most assuredly with the Liberals, though his political connexions are at present with Mr. Disraeli's party) expressing himself thus in speaking on the point of Mr. Gladstone's resolutions as evading the real question, which "real question" is —what is to be done with the property of the Church if it be taken away from her?

"If this were merely matter of verbal criticism I might allude to it in passing, but should do no more, but I think it goes a great deal deeper into the root of the matter than mere verbal criticism. Dis-establishment is one thing, disendowment is another. It is conceivable that a Church might be dis-established, and yet might retain all its endowments. It is equally conceivable that a Church might retain the style and title of an establishment, whatever that may amount to, and yet be so deprived of the bulk of its possessions as to be compelled to rely for its support, in the main, upon the voluntary principle ; and my objection is that while you profess to be laying down a principle, which is to guide the nation in its dealings with the Irish Church, you are touching only a corner of the question, you are avoiding all the real difficulties . . . . The third resolution, whatever its constitutional bearings may be— and there will be something to be said as to the legality of the course to be taken under it—leaves us just as much in the dark as the first, whether the House pledges itself to take away from the Church all its endowments, or half of them, or to leave them all as they are."

Then, after adverting to the various plans, Mr. Miall's for total spoliation ; Mr. Bright's for assigning a certain share to each denomination, and secularising the rest ; Lord Russell's for dividing the proceeds among all denominations according to numbers; the appropriation scheme of 35 years ago; the plan of some Irish churchmen for simply redistributing the endowments throughout the Irish Church so as to get rid of certain scandals; He says—

"You have five, not to say six projects at least, all of them differing in essential principles, each of them irreconcilable with all the rest, all of them supported probably by a respectable minority in the Church; and that is the chaos in which the right honourable gentleman asks us to plunge at a day's notice, when whatever else public opinion may have decided, *it is perfectly clear that it does not see its way as to which of any of these schemes it intends to adopt.*"

But, lastly, we have the testimony of the third person in point of rank, next to the Royal Family, in the realm, a man who owes his position to a Liberal prime minister, and all whose connexions appear to be amongst the Liberal party in Church and State. I mean the Archbishop of York. He gives us his view of the interior feelings of the party with whom he usually acts, in these words:

"Let me assure your Lordships that the great majority which in another place supported the bill were in favour of dis-establishment alone; and, I say of my own knowledge, that several of those who swelled that majority, will cease to swell it the moment they understand that you are going to strip the Irish Church naked, to disendow it as well as disestablish it."

After these testimonies, I will not further occupy space with extracts from the speeches of Lord Carnarvon, the

Duke of Somerset and others. I may, however, notice that by far the ablest pamphlet I have seen in defence of the Irish Church, that by Bishop O'Brien, commences with pointing out the distinction in question. " In what is commonly called 'The Irish Church Question,' there are two distinct, though connected questions involved. The first is, ought any branch of the Reformed Catholic Church to be established in that country? and the second, supposing the first to be answered in the affirmative, is the actual Establishment on so much too large a scale that it may and ought to be considerably reduced? "

Let us now turn to the schemes proposed, or rather indicated, or hinted at, by the leaders of the party, Mr. Bright and Mr. Gladstone. We have Mr. Bright proposing that the Irish Church should, along with the Roman Catholic and the Presbyterian, retain a share of its present endowments; and we have Mr. Gladstone assuming that three-fifths, or perhaps a fraction more of the property, considered as capitalized, will be retained by the Church. Now, however we may dislike their schemes, let us notice that they distinguish between dis-establishment and dis-endowment.

There are two parties, who, on principle, confound or identify dis-establishment and dis-endowment. There is the party of Mr. Disraeli (who in this matter has not yet seemingly commenced the process of party education), who desire to keep the whole political status and revenue of the Irish Church as it is, on the principle of unmitigated Protestant ascendancy; and there is the Liberation Society, who desire complete spoliation, on the principle of the unlawfulness of endowments. These latter, according to Lord Stanley, have even remonstrated with Mr. Bright himself, because he would leave a pittance to the Church.

These two parties are, each on their own principle, or for their own ends, earnestly desirous that we should confound the two things. But anything whatsoever between the two extremes of maintaining everything exactly as it is, and of complete spoliation, gives up the principle. If we keep to the Church of Ireland one quarter, half, or three quarters of its present possessions, it is all the same; the principle involved in the identification of the two is given up, and all becomes simply a matter of detail or degree.

I shall now give my reasons for advocating dis-establishment. I advocate it because it is only a matter of justice to the people of Ireland that we should no longer keep up the solemn farce of proclaiming to the world that Ireland is what it is not.

By keeping up the Establishment of the Anglican Church in Ireland you say to the world that Ireland is Protestant, when you know, and all the world knows, that she is radically Romanist.

In the case of every other nation on the face of the earth, except Ireland, the *bonâ fide* religion of the country, the form of worship in which the bulk of the nation join, and in which the national religious life is embodied, is the form which in that country is held forth as its public profession of religion by being "established." But in Ireland you have the religion of one man in eight blazoned before the world as the religion of the kingdom—you have the religion of a very small minority dignified with all the adjuncts which in the eyes of the world indicate that a religion is established. Its bishops are the only ones who can lawfully assume the title of the bishoprics originally founded by the national missionaries; a portion of them sit by rotation in the senate, and their appointment is considered to be of such national importance that it is entrusted to the highest and most responsible person in the realm; then its priests are the rectors of the parishes into which the whole territory is parcelled out; the decisions of its ecclesiastical courts are enforced by civil penalties; and all state pageants which yet continue to be hallowed by prayer, are so hallowed by its ministers, and within the walls of its sanctuaries. All these appanages are, in the case of every other country, the marks of the religion of the nation; they are, quite apart from endowment, the means by which it asserts its Christianity before the world.

Is it not then grossly unfair (to use the mildest term) to the Irish nation that we should profess for it as if it were its national organ of religion, a form of Christianity which as a nation it repudiates? for surely the fact of the proportion of Romanists to Church of England Protestants in that country being eight to one, and that after three centuries of proscription of the one religion and national encouragement of the other, is on the part of the Irish a most determined repudiation—a repudiation which we may lament with all our souls, but a repudiation which if we would not ignore the truth of facts, we must acknowledge, and which if we allow self government and equality of civil rights, we must take into full political account.

To all this it is rejoined that England and Ireland are one nation, and that the continued establishment of the Irish Church is to be defended on the ground that Ireland is a part of England.

Now it is quite true that there is a political unity called the United Kingdom, but it is equally true that this kingdom consists of three nations, each having its separate national character, national history, national traditions, and national religious life, and there is no power on earth capable of making them one nation. You may as well think by an act of Parliament to make fire and water the same, as imagine by such a thing as an act of Parliament to make any two nations one. All the powers of such a despotic government as Austria was, could not weld the congeries of nations composing the Austrian empire into one nation, though they all seem loyal to one sovereign and profess one religion.

Even politically we have in many ways to treat England and Ireland separately : for instance, most acts of Parliament do not refer to Ireland, except there is a special provision. In the matter of Reform they were dealt with separately.

And so with the three kingdoms; an act of Parliament may make them a political unity, but upon all matters so touching their national life as their profession of religion, they must each be dealt with separately; if we are to have an united kingdom in anything but the

name. We have had so to deal with Scotland. We
have had to allow her to express her religious life, or
what she thinks to be such, in her own way, and we
must mete the same measure to Ireland. At least the
precedent of our treatment of Scotland makes the
measure which we mete to Ireland seem at least to be
flagrantly unjust.

This matter of the *establishment* on the part of England of Protestantism in Ireland is, it appears to me,
far more galling than its endowment, for it is equivalent
to this, that England treats Scotland as of full age and
able to "think for herself," and "answer for herself,"
whilst the same England insists on treating Ireland as
an infant, and, as her godmother, steps forth before the
world and answers in her name. Now just in proportion
as the profession of sectarian differences is made of
paramount importance, so will the profession on our
part of a religion for the Irish, be intolerable to
them. A nation which has conquered them, and over
and over again confiscated their land, takes upon
itself to profess for them a form of Christianity which
they abhor. We treat a nation as old and as proud,
and (in its way) more religious than ourselves, as in a
state of nonage with regard to religion, and yet having
irritated this same nation to the utmost with our
unmeaning officiousness, we treat her politically as our
equal, and give her 100 seats in our House of Commons,
so enabling her to hold the balance between our two
great parties, and to make her own terms with our legislature.

This seems the place to advert for a moment to the use constantly made of the truism that *numbers are no test of truth,* from which we are asked to infer that a nation is not to take numbers into account in determining the relations betwixt itself and its religion. But a nation is made up of numbers, its mode of existence is in one sense numerical; and let us carefully remember that all else besides mere numbers which goes to form a nation, such as national feeling, traditions, distinction of race, even language, is in this case against the Irish Church. It is the Church of the English in Ireland rather than of the native Irish.

But the English nation establishes the Irish Church as a Missionary Church, If so, she is not only the most unsuccessful, but the most anomalous Missionary Church in the world, and that from the fact of her being *established.*

In every other case a Missionary Church is an aggressive body, working in some heathen land to supplant a heathen establishment; and she takes the form of an establishment by ceasing to become missionary. This has actually taken place in more than one mission of the Church Missionary Society.

When a district has been so far Christianized that the parochial system can be worked in it as in this country, that Society has withdrawn its missionary action from it and transferred it to fields beyond : and this I believe the Church Missionary Society has done with the express purpose of keeping itself a purely missionary society, as distinguished from a society aiding establishments or quasi establishments. If, however, we employ this "Missionary" argúment we must do so honestly and consistently, for surely the one great business of a missionary Church is to proselytize, and the advocates of the Irish Church both in and out of Parliament have deprecated her dis-establishment on the express ground that if dis-established she will become more aggressive and proselytizing.

It is very Irish logic to argue that she should continue established on the missionary ground, because, if dis-established she will at once begin to take missionary ground, and act as a missionary body is expected to do.

But it is objected that if the State ceases to establish Protestantism in Ireland, it will cease to recognize the truth of the Gospel. Now what is here meant by the state? If England alone is meant, then I assert most solemnly that England cannot recognize the truth for Ireland. Ireland must recognize it for herself. Before her own Master, the Judge of nations, she will have to stand or fall alone. By no possible theory of imputation, legal or evangelical, can the Protestantism of England be imputed to a country so irretrievably Popish. The righteous King of nations cannot possibly demand such a fiction.

But if by the State be meant the three nations, then Ireland is one of three numerically, and she must be assumed to be equal to the smaller and far less populous kingdom of Scotland; so that she should have her own word respecting her own profession ; or at least, the first and most powerfnl of the three should not take upon itself to profess for her.

Before concluding this part of the subject I shall
examine briefly:—

1. The bearing on this matter of the religious
statistics of Ireland.

2. The Question :—Is the present Church of Ireland
the representative of the ancient Church of St. Patrick?

1. The denominational statistics of Ireland.

According to the census of 1861, the population of
Ireland was as follows:—

Established Church	693,357
Roman Catholics	4,505,265
Presbyterians	523,291
Other Protestant Dissenters ..	72,054
	5,793,967

So that there is in Ireland one Churchman to between
six and seven Roman Catholics, one Protestant to nearly
four Roman Catholics—and one Churchman to somewhat
above seven of all other denominations.

These proportions, however, are by no means the same
throughout the country.

Throughout the whole island the Church numbers
11.9 per cent of the population, whereas in

Ulster	she numbers	20.4	per cent.
Leinster	„	12.39	
Munster	„	5.3	
Connaught	„	4.44	

Taking counties the Church population ranges between

Fermanagh	38 per cent.
Armagh	30 „
Tyrone	21 „
Down	20 „

Dublin, Wicklow, Antrim, and Londonderry } 15 to 20.

King's County, Queen's County, Cavan, Carlow, Kildare, Donegal, and Monaghan } 10 to 15.

Longford, Louth, Meath, Westmeath, Wexford, Cork, Tipperary, Leitrim, and Sligo } 5 to 10

Kilkenny, Limerick, Tipperary, Kerry Roscommon } 3 to 5.

Waterford, Galway, Mayo .. 2 to 3.

Clare .. 2.

The Presbyterians, who are Scotch colonists, are almost all crowded together in the northern province, where in the populous counties of Antrim and Down, they outnumber the Roman Catholics and Church people (taken separately); but in the three other provinces they are very insignificant, so that in these latter the population for all practical purposes may be divided into Romanist and Anglican. These statistics are assumed on all sides to be correct. They certainly are not impugned in pamphlets written on the side of the Irish Church.

Now I desire earnestly to impress upon the reader that nothing whatsoever can destroy, or in the long run, even weaken the force of these statistics.

You may see put forward long lists of parishes containing far larger numbers of Church people than an ordinary English parish; but after all the fact remains that in the comparatively small county of Fermanagh, where the Church is strongest, she does not number anything like half the population, and in the vast districts where she is weakest she does not amount to three per cent. In the most Protestant province she only numbers 20 per cent., and in the most Romanist only 5 per cent.

Every manipulation of statistics which, allowing the accuracy of these government returns, would make out a stronger case for her, does so by suppressing a material part of the whole truth of the matter. I will give an illustration.

In a tract I have now before me, purporting to be an extract from a charge delivered by the Archdeacon of Lindisfarne, the following statement is made on the authority of Lord Cairns. "The average income of each incumbent is £280, the average number of members of the Church in town parishes is 1590 souls, and in rural parishes 376. A country parish in Ireland averages 20 square miles. In England the average income of each incumbent is £285, the average population of a rural parish in England is 387 members of the Church, and in Wales 248, and the average area of an English country parish is only five square miles."

Now this seems to prove the churches of England and Ireland to be in the same position as to their re spective populations: indeed, taking into consideration the area of Irish parishes, the advantage is on the side of the Church in Ireland; but let us read it in the light of the fact that throughout Ireland the proportion of Romanist to Anglican is 7 to 1.

Thus the average number of Church people in town parishes being 1590 *in a country throughout which the Church is only one eighth* of the population, then these same parishes have an average population of 12,720, of which only 1590 are Church people. Again the average number in rural parishes being 376, these same parishes must, (taking the average proportion throughout the country of Romanist and Anglicans into account) have each a population of somewhat above 3000, of whom only 376 are Anglicans.

But this is by no means all, for the average English parish is five square miles, whereas the average country benefice in Ireland is twenty square miles; so that to get an average Church population of only 376, we have to combine as a parish an area of twenty square miles.

Whatever this be, it is certainly not that parochial system which we have always looked upon as inherent in the idea of an establishment

Take another case. The opponents of the Irish Church put out a statement that there were 199 parishes in Ireland without Protestants. The advocates of the Church met this with the counter statement that there were only 18 benefices without Protestants.

The facts of the case are now well known, and are simply these. The ecclesiastical benefice is in many cases

an union of two or more civil parishes, so that there may
be 199 civil parishes more or less without Protestants,
whilst there are only 20 ecclesiastical benefices so situated.

But on which side does the very correction tell?
Evidently against the Establishment of the Irish Church;
for, in order to get a Protestant population in these 199
parishes, we have to join two or more civil parishes
of far larger area than an average English parish. In
order to supply an Irish benefice or ecclesiastical parish
with Protestants, you have to join together as one parish,
what amounts to five English parishes. Any parochial
sub-division into parishes of workable size will not afford
Protestants, and we have to unite as unions or ecclesiastical benefices large districts of country, one of which,
according to Bishop O'Brien, is larger than the county
of Rutland by no less than 80,000 acres, and his Lord-
ship adds the remark, "it is no doubt a remarkable
though by no means an unique case."

As the reader may think that there is some mistake
in the figures I will give the account in Bishop O'Brien's
own words.

"The benefice was a union of two parishes, Kilcommon Erris containing 203,396 acres, and Kilmore Erris
containing 29,493 acres. The whole union (i.e. Ecclesiastical Benefice,) therefore contained 232,709 acres.
Kilcommon Erris is 30 miles long and 18½ wide, its
area, as given above, is 203,396 acres. Louth (Irish
county) is 25 miles long by 15 in its greatest breadth,
and the area 201,434 acres. Rutlandshire is 18 miles
by 15, and its area 128,000 acres. The smaller parish

was the one retained by my friend (he is speaking of their division into two benefices), and though it was of so much more moderate dimensions than the other, being only 17 miles long by 5 in its greatest breadth, it had some peculiarities which made it very certain that no one who worked it honestly was eating the bread of idleness." Again "Ballinakill, in the diocese of Tuam, was 40 Irish miles long by 20 miles wide (more than 50 miles by 25 English), and comprehended besides, four islands, one of these more than 17 Irish (more than 21 English) miles long. It is now divided, I believe, into six parishes." So that taking the average breadth of this Ballinakill as only 12 English miles, each of these six parishes (!) was above 100 square miles in extent.

Again, from a note in the next page it appears that in many cases the parishes which make up the union are not contiguous, and that the parts of the single parish are widely separated. Here is the case of a single parish, Derryvollan, diocese of Clogher, of which it is said in the Report—"the length and breadth of this parish cannot be stated, it consisting of two distinct portions, at an *interval of six* miles distant, with two detached townlands in the space intervening." In Kilpeacon, diocese of Limerick, it is said that one of the three parishes of which the union consists, is thirteen miles from the others. And in another, Kilflynn, diocese of Ardfert, it is noticed—"the first four parishes are contiguous, and distant about thirty miles from the remaining members of the Union. From some tables before me I see Kilflynn has 97 church population, and Kilpeacon 38; but Derryvollan has 3,176.

I shall again advert to these cases, for in proportion as they tell in favour of the dis-establishment, as a national Church, of a Church which is obliged to retain so anomalous a parochial system, they tell against its spoliation.

We have now briefly to consider the question :—Is the Imperial Parliament bound to keep the Church of Ireland in its present status as a National Church because it is the rightful representative of the ancient National Church of Ireland? But if this ground is taken where are we to stop? I do not say that it is likely, but it is still within the verge of possibility, that the Irish Church, by emigration or by the inroads of Popery on the one side and Protestant Dissent on the other, may diminish still more in numbers, so that instead of numbering one in eight, she should number one in fifty, her present numerical proportion in one county (Clare) ; is she still to be considered the religious educator of the nation, and the public expression of its religious belief?

But not to insist on this, let us consider what amount of certainty there is in the assertion that the present Church of Ireland represents, or is, the ancient National Church of St. Patrick. That she should fairly represent the ancient Church of Ireland depends upon four things :

1. Similarity of doctrine.
2. Similarity of ecclesiastical government and discipline.
3. Episcopal succession, traceable to the primitive
   Irish Church.
4. Birth and extraction.

1. Similarity of doctrine is most important, but alone it cannot prove the identity of any existing ecclesiastical corporation with one existing in early ages, for granting fully that St. Patrick was, so far as his relations with the Bishop of Rome were concerned, all that the most zealous Protestant can wish; and that, as some most interesting remains clearly show, he held salvation by Christ alone, rejecting all Popish mediation of the Virgin and saints, still, taking doctrine alone into account, the Presbyterians and other Protestant sects represent on these points the doctrine of St. Patrick as fully as the Church can possibly do.

2. As to similarity of ecclesiastical government I am afraid, if Dr Wordsworth gives us a true view of the state of the case, that this proof of identity must be given up altogether, for according to him (Dr. W.) the original Church of St. Patrick was neither diocesan nor parochial. His words are, " she (the ancient Irish Church) did not follow the example of the ancient churches of Christ. She did not walk according to their order and rule; she had pastors without flocks, bishops without dioceses.". . . " She had many bishops, but these bishops had no dioceses. Many of them lived in collegiate and monastic institutions. The spiritual pre-eminence of these bishops was acknowledged, but their episcopal functions were exercised under the direction of the heads of those institutions. We should have a parallel case in England if our bishops were drawn out of their dioceses, and if the members of the Episcopate were absorbed into our cathedrals and colleges, and if their Episcopal minis-

trations in ordaining and confirming were to be placed under the control of the deans of our cathedrals and of the heads of our colleges. Monasticism domineered over Episcopacy in Ireland, and to such a degree did this anomaly prevail that in some instances, where a woman was at the head of the conventual institution, *the bishop acted as her subaltern.* This was the case at Kildare. The Bishop of Kildare was the nominee and functionary of the Abbess St. Bridget and her successors (! !)."

Incredible as all this may appear, there seems to be no doubt of its truth. The writer of a learned review in the Christian Remembrancer for July, 1864, gives other instances—"The abbots of Hi, who in imitation of their founder, St. Columba, were only priests, had under their jurisdiction the whole province, bishops included." It is clear that no Church in existence represents such a state of things as regards Church government as that which prevailed in the early Irish Church.

3. But we have now to approach a far more "vexed" question. "Is the present Established Church of Ireland the true and rightful representative, by Episcopal succession, of the early Irish Church?" Here I feel I am treading not only on delicate, but on the most uncertain ground. The facts which, as far as I can see, cannot be impugned, are these:—

The succession of the whole Irish Episcopate from the time of the accession of Elizabeth to the Restoration, is derived from Hugh Curwin, Archbishop of

Dublin on the accession of Queen Elizabeth, so far as this, that he was the original Protestant consecrator, and the whole controversy raised by Dr. Brady's pamphlet merely turns on this, whether he was assisted by Irish bishops or not.

Curwin was an Englishman, and had received deacon's and priest's, as well as his episcopal orders, in the Church of England. His consecrators were Edmund Bonner, Bishop of London, Thomas Thirlby, Bishop of Ely, and Maurice Griffin, Bishop of Rochester. He is the only bishop whose name has come down to us as having consecrated Craike, Bishop of Kildare, the first Protestant bishop consecrated after the accession of Elizabeth. He is also the only bishop whose name has come down to us as having consecrated Loftus, Archbishop of Armagh, the second Protestant Irish bishop consecrated in Queen Elizabeth's reign. The third and fourth Protestant bishops, Hugh Brady of Meath, and Robert Daly of Kildare, both derived their succession from Curwin and Loftus. No other names are recorded as having consecrated them.

So that so far as regards Episcopal succession the name of Curwin is all important, and his succession is English, not Irish. So that any Irish or national element in the succession of the present Establishment must have come from those who are supposed to have assisted him, whose names have not come down to us.

The first question is, have we reason to believe that Curwin was assisted by other bishops in consecrating Craike and Loftus? The reader is of course aware of the controversy that there has been within the last few years on this subject; most writers in defence of the Irish Establishment, maintaining that the bishops at the commencement of the reign of Elizabeth conformed in a body to the reformed religion, and so would assist Curwin in transmitting the ancient succession; whilst against this it has been urged by Dr. Maziere Brady that almost all of them died Papists, and so were not likely to have assisted; and that Elizabeth's power was so weak beyond the pale that she could not compel their services.

After a careful consideration of the facts adduced by Dr. Maziere Brady on the one side, and the pamphlets in answer by Archdeacons Stopford and Lee on the other, the state of the case appears to be this : Dr. Brady appears to have much understated the influence of the Elizabethan government without the pale. The evidence also which he gives from Roman documents, transcribed by Romanists, that a large proportion of the Irish bishops died in full communion with the Romish Church seems to me singularly weak, insufficient, and unreliable. It appears to me that most of them played a double game —they endeavoured to hold both to the Pope and to Queen Elizabeth, and they apparently, most of them, succeeded, for Elizabeth counted on their loyalty and employed them even against their own nation whilst they lived, and the Pope blessed their memory after their death.

The question, however, is, had Elizabeth sufficient influence to induce or to compel them to take part in the Consecration of a Protestant Bishop according to the Reformed Ritual? The Bishop of Down and Connor,

Magennis, would certainly have done so. The Bishop of Ardagh, Patrick Mc. Mahon, would have done so. It is very probable that Elizabeth had a bishop willing to assist in the Bishop of Kilmore. Bishop Field of Leighlin also undoubtedly conformed, and Patrick Walsh of Waterford and Lismore seems also to have been a Protestant. The proof of adherence to the Papacy on the part of Skiddy, of Cork, is slender in the extreme; in fact there does not seem to have been any lack of Protestant bishops to assist Curwin. Whether they actually took part with him depends upon whether their assistance was considered necessary by the government. When Archdeacons Lee and Stopford assume that queen Elizabeth's government must necessarily have acted in accordance with the canons requiring three bishops to assist at a consecration, we cannot help remembering that the canons respecting age were deliberately broken through in the case of Loftus, the first Protestant Archbishop of Armagh, who was consecrated at the uncanonical age of twenty-eight. There is, it seems to me, abundant proof that the medieval Church continually disregarded the canon respecting the presence of three bishops.

But I desire to direct the reader's attention to this point—supposing that we could distinctly prove that Curwin was assisted by other Irish bishops, that would only connect the present with the pre-reformation, or medieval Church, so far as Episcopal succession is concerne d; for, be it remembered, that the Apostolical or Episcopal succession of the Church of Ireland for many years before the Reformation must have been essentially English. One single page of Archdeacon Stopford's answer to Dr. Brady affords abundant proof of this. In page 21 we have records of the consecration of six bishops to sees in Ireland, and all of them by bishops in England. These are given as specimens of any number and from an extract given respecting the last, it appears to have been the rule—for the king obliged them to be consecrated in England, in order that he might compel them to renounce in person the clause prejudicial to the crown always thrust into the Pope's bull of consecration.

It is clear that any connexion by way of succession from the early Irish Church, must have been, at the time of the Reformation, reduced to a minimum, if not extinguished altogether.

The state of the case then is this. Archbishop Curwin, the consecrator, transmitted only English succession, and the succession of those who assisted him, if any, must have been mainly English; so that any connection by Episcopal succession of Bishops Craike and Loftus, with the ancient national Church of Ireland, must have been infinitesimal.

With regard to the fourth point of connection by which the present Church of Ireland may be said to be the rightful national heir of the original Church, I would draw attention to these facts.

From a table given by Archdeacon Stopford of the bishops of the Irish Church from the Conquest to the Reformation, 292 are Englishmen, 261 Irish, and 128 doubtful.

2. From tables given by Bishop Mant, it appears that out of 13 archbishops of Armagh, from Henry VIII. to the Revolution, 8 were Englishmen ; of 9 archbishops of Dublin, 7 were English ; of 13 bishops of Down and Connor, 6 were English, 3 Scotchmen, and 2 doubtful; of 6 bishops of Dromore (alone), 4 were English; of 9 bishops of Derry, not one was an Irishman ; of 10 archbishops of Armagh from the Revolution to the present time, 8 were English; of 14 archbishops of Dublin, 9 were English.

So far then as birth and parentage are concerned, the present Irish Establishment is far more English than Irish. This of course is not its fault, but it must be no less treated as a fact in any attempt to resettle its relations with the Irish nation.

And now I have to proceed to consider the second proposition I laid down at the outset, which is, that the wholesale disendowment of the Anglican church in Ireland would be a grievous wrong to a section of the people of Ireland, on whose loyalty this country has relied for above 300 years for enabling her to keep her hold upon Ireland, and without whose aid that island would not now be a part of the British Empire. Before entering upon details let me remind the reader that no leading Liberal of the smallest weight (except Mr. Miall), has advocated the total disendowment of the Irish Church; and I have brought forward at the commencement sufficient proof from the published utterances of various men of mark in that party to shew that any such proposal would break up the party. Now, if the smallest endowment be retained, the only *principle* on which wholesale confiscation can be defended, is given up. The Liberation Society insist on confiscation on principle—the principle that all endowments are wrong. But Mr. Bright himself when he proposed that of the property of the Irish Establishment, some should be given to Roman Catholics, some to the Church, some to Presbyterians, and the rest secularised, gave up the principle. So, of course, has Mr. Gladstone in the propositions which he made respecting the glebes, the parsonages, the fabrics of the churches, and the vested interests of patrons. So that on all hands it is allowed that the dis-endowment is to be, not a matter of principle, but of circumstances, and of degree.

Let us now consider this question :—Have the Protestants of Ireland any claims that in their case, disendowment, if dis-endowment to some extent there is to be (and I, for one, look upon it as inevitable), should be mitigated as much as possible—in fact that it should be minimized? Are there considerations, historical and national, why Mr. Gladstone, if it turn out that he is to have the management of this question, should be held to his own words, interpreted in the largest sense of liberality to the Irish Church. "This is the point at issue, that the Church in Ireland should cease to exist as an establishment, though with every softening measure that a due regard to proprietary and vested interests, and I would add, even to feelings, can suggest."

Is there any peculiar reason why, in this case, these vested interests should not be merely the monetary interests of patrons, but the spiritual interests of flocks;

that these spiritual interests should not be left to the voluntary principle, *in cases where that principle has most signally failed?* I think that the whole past history, as well as the present state of Ireland, presents us with such reasons. For " The Irish Question " is two-fold. It is a land, as well as a church question. When certain Liberal politicians assert that the Irish Church is at the bottom of all the heart-burnings which exist between the two countries, they assert what they must know to be very wide of the truth—what the united voice of all the organs of genuine Irish and Roman Catholic opinion shew to be wide of the truth.

For the master grievance of the Romish Celtic population of Ireland is that the land is in the hands of a Protestant proprietary. The Church grievance is very subordinate to this. Now Protestant proprietorship in the land has meant, since the time of Queen Elizabeth, and yet means, the possession of Ireland by the British Crown. If in the days of Elizabeth and her successors, the proprietorship of land in Ireland had been in Romish or Celtic hands, the existence of England as an independent Protestant state would have been imperilled, for Ireland could never have existed as an independent king-dom. She would have been in the hands of France, and what chance, humanly speaking, would England have had with Romanist France on the one side, and Ireland virtually, if not actually, belonging to France, and commanding all the British coasts from Bristol to Glasgow, on the other.

This is what is called Protestant ascendancy. Till within the last century and a-half, when the nations of

Europe ceased to fight among themselves under the two banners of Catholic and Protestant, it actually involved the possession of Ireland. Till within the last century, *i.e.*, up to the times of the repeal of the penal laws and of Catholic emancipation, it consisted of two things, civil and ecclesiastical ascendancy. The civil aspect of Protestant ascendancy consisted not merely of proprietorship in the land, but the absolute monopoly of all political privileges, so that Protestants only could vote either in Parliament or out of it.

Now, just as civil ascendancy consisted of both Protestant proprietorship and Protestant exclusive privileges, so ecclesiastical ascendancy consisted of two things, the Protestant clergy holding certain property, and also certain exclusive privileges, which privileges constituted the "establishment" of the church. Just then as the monopoly of civil privileges by Protestants has been given up, so must the ecclesiastical privileges answering to these, *i.e.*, establishment. But just as with the cessation of Protestant monopoly of civil rights, Protestant proprietorship did not cease, so neither ought Protestant proprietorship of certain Church property of necessity to cease with dis-establishment.

The giving up of whatsoever constitutes Establishment in the Irish Church is equivalent to the surrender on the part of the Protestant laity of their electoral and other exclusive priviledges, but as the surrender of these on the part of the laity was not accompanied with any confiscation of their estates, so ought the question of the surrender of the exclusive privileges of the Protestant Church, as an establishment, to be considered quite apart from the spoliation of its ecclesiastical property. The Irish difficulty has been since the time of the conquest of Ireland, a land or proprietorship difficulty, only since the Reformation h.s it been a religious difficulty.* The endowment and support of the Protestant Church has been vastly subsidiary to the maintenance of Protestant proprietorship, *i.e.*, of British hold upon Ireland.

All this seems to me to tell in favour of some continued endowment of the Protestant Church, or at least, makes anything like its total disendowment a most iniquitous matter on the part of the British Government.

When it is thrown in the teeth of the Irish Church that she is a "garrison Church," I reply that that is just what (in three provinces at least) she has been, and is; and it is this very thing which entitles her to the fullest possible consideration in dealing with her revenues.

* Let it be remembered that the Irish difficulty is, in fact, the difficulty of "civilisation" itself. Before the time of the conquest of Ireland there was no civilisation, because there was no property in land. The ancestors of the O'Donoghues and O'Gradys of our day, were like the savages of New Zealand; each tribe had its territory, but no individual of the tribe had any property in the common estate or territory. Moreover, the headship of the tribe was not hereditary but elective, so that every barony or townland in Ireland was a sort of little Poland—tho moment a chief expired the headship of the clan had to be fought for; and every man of mark in the tribe had been for years preparing for his chance by attaching to himself all the blood-thirsty villains he could contrive to keep in his pay. The early history of Ireland is consequently such as the history of New Zealand or North America would have been, had it been committed to writing; raids, massacres, burnings, and nothing else. So that it is literally true that "all property in Ireland is the creation of some English king." If the reader desires to pursue this subject further let him order Mr. Hobart Seymour's interesting pamphlet, entitled "Ten Years in the Irish Church."

We may abominate much in the past policy of England, but what could she do? Could she possibly have suffered such a state of continuous anarchy, inviting the interference of all Europe, in a land conterminous to her own?

For what, I ask, has been the "garrison"? Not a garrison safe behind entrenchments, but a million of Protestants, men, women and children, scattered over an open country, which in no invidious sense, but in a sense which the native Irish themselves would be the first to acknowledge, must be called an enemy's country, maintaining amidst difficulties and dangers unparalleled a loyalty which has saved the Empire : for I suppose that no one would be hardy enough to say that we should have retained Ireland if this garrison of Protestants had not been loyal in the face of plunder, burning, and massacre.

Of course I do not mean for one moment to assert that the burning, plunder, and massacre has been all on one side. Ireland has been from the time of the conquest till some way into the present century in a chronic state of war, with intervals of *truce*, but no interval of *peace*. God forbid that any minister of Christ should defend oppression and misgovernment, but when men talk of past ages of misgovernment do they mean to assert that England should have relaxed her hold upon Ireland, and have allowed her to become an appanage of some Roman Catholic European power; for that Ireland would ever have held her own as an independent state no one in his senses can believe.

The Church of Ireland is undoubtedly a garrison Church. Well, then, the radical secularist rejoins, Let the garrison pay for their own Church. To which the garrison answers, " We do," for the Protestant Church is supported almost entirely by Protestant proprietors; and the amount paid by Roman Catholic landlords exactly equals the sum paid back to their Church in the shape of the Maynooth Grant. But it is rejoined, is not the payment of tithes to the Protestant clergy a payment in such a shape that it must be looked upon as a national payment?

To which it is replied that the Protestant clergy have not the tithes. They have, I believe, little more than their share if the whole amount of tithe were collected and divided between Catholics and Protestants, according to their numbers, for in Ireland the so-called tithe does not bear anything like the same relation to the whole produce, which it does in this country.*

This, which I do not see noticed by writers or speakers on either side of the question, seems to bear very materially on the question of disendowment as a national matter; for the Irish Church is not in the position of a national Church which as such (i.e. by national arrangement or gift) has a right to the full tithe. She is already disendowed to a very great extent, in fact to such an extent that, as I said, if the national right to the full tithe were to be asserted, in order that it might be divided amongst all denominations, the Church would, in such a division, retain pretty nearly its present quota of the whole tenth. A Church which retains only one sixth of that which is assumed to be national property devoted to the maintenance of religion certainly does not seem to offend very grievously.

---

* It was proved before a Select Committee of the House of Commons in 1832, by the highest authority in Ireland, Sir R. Griffith, that the whole amount of tithe composition was less than one-sixtieth of the produce of the land, that is to say, one sixth of the amount to which the clergy are supposed to have a legal right.

If the whole Irish question be, as is so often said, a matter of feeling, the susceptibilities of the Irish character cannot be wounded by the Protestant Church retaining so small a part of the endowments of an establishment, at least to anything like the degree that they are wounded by the same Church retaining the dignities and status of an establishment.

And now let us look at the question of disendowment in detail. Unless there is to be confiscation on the principle of the Liberation Society, (*i. e.* for mere confiscation's sake,) the whole matter of disendowment is a matter of detail. So one of the most advanced and far seeing of the Liberal party tells us in his speech to his constituents at Bradford. Mr. Forster there says, "It will be impossible to enter into detail upon the point. It will be necessary, I expect, to have some commission of enquiry to settle that."*

If we are to deal justly with the Protestant population of Ireland the case of each parish, so far as disendowment is concerned, must be judged on its own merits.

I desire to draw attention to the following facts. The Bishop of Oxford, in his speech in the House of Lords on the Suspensory Bill, makes this statement, which we may assume to be correct, "I hold in my hand at this moment a list of 22 parishes in Ireland, the Church population of which varies from 8,000 to 1,000, and the revenues, including pew rents, from £188 the highest, to £89 per annum the lowest." If the revenues of such

* The same is allowed by Mr. A. W. Peel, at Warwick; and notably by Sir Roundell Palmer; and, as far as I can understand his speech, by Lord Bury, at Berwick; and many others.

parishes arc to bc confiscated it can only bc for confiscation's sake. I takc, of course, thesc parishes as presenting both in respect of income and population extrcme cases.

We shall next refer to some information from a very diffcrent source. It is a table given in a book by Mr. Skeats, published by the Liberation Society, professing to give the income and population of all the benefices whose incumbents receive above £400 per annum. These are in all about 216 out of 1,500. Of these 64, or nearly onc-third of these more valuable livings, have above 1,000 Protestants; 41 have between 500 and 1,000, and 17 between 400 and 500. Taking into consideration the scattered nature of the population of Irish parishes it is clear that by far the grcater part of these "best livings" of the Irish Church are no sinecures. It is no sinecure to have to look after the spiritual interests of a thousand persons, scattered over ecclesiastical benefices having an average of 20 square miles in extent, and in a country so uncivilized. If such livings are despoiled a very gross injustice will be done, and an injustice doubly gross in the case of a country like England, which has had to rely in times past for her political existence in no small degree on the maintenance of this "garrison," whose spiritual interests she is now asked to leave to chance.

Whilst this pamphlet has been in preparation the Report of the Irish Church Commissioners has come out.

Schedule V. gives the benefices of thc Church of Ireland, their area, Protestant population, incomc, and its sources and outgoings.

I extract from it the following cases in point.

Name of Parish.	Protestant Population.	Extent in Acres.	Page of Report.
Clonfeacle	1778	13,000	114
Kildross	1080	24,000	124
Aghalurcher	2397	30,000	138
Agharea	2162	17,000	138
Cleenish	2940	26,000	140
Clogher	1860	19,000	140
Clones	4492	42,000	142
Cloontibret	590	21,000	142
Devenish	1500	30,000	144
Errigle Trough	548	24,000	146
Findonagh	1978	17,000	146
Inishmacsaint	1891	19,000	148
Mullaghfad	502	17,000	152
Tydavnet	850	35,000	154
Enniskeen	457	20,000	166
Fercall	717	34,000	166
Lower Badoney	848	47,000	188
Upper Badoney	512	38,000	188
Maghera	1144	22,000	204
Donagheady	1087	31,000	196
Donaghmore	1284	46,000	196
Termona Mongan	1108	45,000	208
Clondehorkey	1266	30,400	210
Clonderaddock	694	27,000	210
Killybegs	425	26,000	214
Kiltevogue	675	41,000	216
Templecrone	495	52,000	220
Tullyaughnish	621	16,000	220
Tullaghobigley	301	68,000	220
Skerry	776	60,000	254
Moyntagh	1446	18,000	262
Kilkeel	3816	80,000	264
Swanlinbar	983	25,000	280
Templeport	821	42,000	280
Boyle	844	33,000	284
Kilkeevin	560	48,000	286
Clongish	1047	35,000	294
Cloon	817	42,000	294
Castlebar	462	105,000	304
Kilcummin	288	98,006	308
Kiltullagh	399	67,000	312
Rahoon	605	57,000	314
Westport	534	156,000	314
Kilmoremoy	908	75,000	318

Want of space alone prevents me from citing double the number of parishes like the above. The schedule occupies 450 pages. The above instances are culled from not above half. The reader will observe that every one of the above parishes has a population of upwards of 300 scattered over more than 25 square miles of land; in by far the majority of cases above 35 square miles, i. e., above eight times the area of an average English parish. I have also designedly excluded all parishes containing towns of any size, or parts of such towns, because I desire to impress upon the reader the iniquity of throwing such parishes as the above on the tender mercies of the Voluntary system. The Voluntary principle may be successful in large towns, but in a scattered country population it utterly fails, so that it is not true to say that if the Irish Church is disendowed she will be simply put into the position of all sects depending upon the Voluntary principle. She will be thrown for her maintenance upon ground which the voluntary sects never choose to occupy, which they always refuse as utterly unremunerative, and which has failed in maintaining anything like an educated ministry even in America, the home of Voluntaryism.

I repeat again, if the Irish Protestant population is to be dealt with justly, the case of each parish must be dealt with separately. For instance, it appears to me that it would scarcely be a boon to the Protestants of such parishes as the above, to retain, as Mr. Gladstone proposes, the parsonage house, glebe, and in some cases, the church. The retention of such things would serve to localise a ministry which ought to be as much on an itinerant footing as the ministry in our most sparsely peopled colonies. For such places as Kiltevogue, Kilcummin, and Tullaghobigley, the vicarage *horse* seems a far more fitting institution than the vicarage *house.*

Such a table of livings and their areas as I have given, tells, it seems to me, with equal force against the continued establishment of an institution which is obliged to lump together such tracts of country in order to make a Protestant population for a benefice, and against its total dis-endowment, or rather spoliation; for how can such scattered populations maintain their own ministers? The Protestant sects for the most part give up the case as hopeless.

But are not the landlords mostly Church of England? Yes, after a sort; but they already pay their quota in the shape of tithes to the maintenance of religion. These they must continue to pay, and they who know them best think that there is not much more to be got out of them. It is to be remembered that the 500, 600 or 700 persons in these parishes of 50,000 acres, are by no means all landlords. There is not much of a respectable Protestant farmer or yeoman class in Galway or Tipperary to maintain a minister even in decent poverty; so the clergyman, when the landlord will consider it worth while to keep one, bids fair to be much in the position of an upper servant. But, it may be rejoined, does not the poor Celt pay his priest, and that liberally? Yes, but be it remembered that the priest has a screw in reserve, the use of which the Protestant pastor more than repudiates. The Church of Ireland in the fervour of its Ultra-Protestant zeal has gone to the verge of what is decent in disparaging her two sacraments, whilst the priest can get his own price for his entire seven. The priest too has the the whole farmer class to work upon, for, as Mr. Skeats informs us in his pamphlet, there are 337,419 Roman Catholic farmers to 45,838 who are members of the Establishment. So that if we except the case of a few large towns there is, in three provinces, absolutely no Protestant middle class, the class whose presence is essential to the working of the voluntary system.

It remains now to conclude the matter by a few remarks on the bearing of the question of the disestablishment of the Church of Ireland on that of the Church of England.

One cannot help being struck with the earnestness with which the advocates of Mr. Gladstone's resolutions deprecate the idea that, in seeking the disestablishment of the Church of Ireland, they have secret ulterior designs on the Church of England. One after another expresses his conviction that the churches stand in entirely different relations to their respective nationalities. And, on the other hand, one cannot help being struck with the pertinacity with which the advocates of the continued establishment of the Irish Church insist on doing the work of the Liberation Society by dragging down the Church of England to the level of the Church of Ireland.

Believing that the Church of England, both in respect of numerical preponderance, historical associations and comprehensiveness, has the best possible title to be upheld as the national profession of the religion of England, and that the Church of Ireland on not one of these grounds has any such title as regards Ireland, I shall briefly give my reasons for believing, not only that the disestablishment of the Irish Church ought not to be followed by that of the Church of England, but that it is not in the least likely that it will be so followed.

The Church in Ireland is the Church of about one in seven or eight of the population of Ireland. This fact is ascertained because the religious profession of each person in Ireland is asked when the civil census is taken. It is impossible to ascertain the numbers of the adherents of the Church of England as compared with Dissenters, because the Dissenters of England, at the time of taking the last census, successfully resisted the only means by which the relative proportions of Church people and Dissenters can be exactly arrived at, viz : by enquiring of each man what his religious profession is. A means, be it remembered, which they consider quite justifiable in the case of Ireland, and rely on its results in their arguments against the Church of Ireland. We can, consequently, only approximate towards the relative proportion of Churchmen and Dissenters in this country.

At the census of 1851 the numbers attending places of worship of all sorts were, in the morning, when by far the greatest number of places were open,

2,371,732 attending Church.
2,056,606 attending all other places of worship whatsoever.

The morning is unquestionably the only time of attendance which can in the least degree be considered a test of a man's religious persuasion.

The attendance at evening service affords no proof of attachment to any body of Christians, and more especially from the fact that of the 11,794 places of worship belonging then to the Church of England, only 2,439 were opened in the evening. Any returns of persons attending evening services may be dismissed as utterly misleading; first, because in country parishes scarcely any churches were open in the evening; and secondly, because (as I have abundant evidence to shew) the greatest possible exertions were made to fill the places open on that Sunday evening, with persons who would have occupied places in the churches if they had been open. I believe that far more than half the congregations on the Sunday evening in question, throughout the country districts, were composed of professing Church people. The attendance on the morning of that day, shews a decided, but not a large majority of persons attending church; but this alone would give a very defective view of the state of the case, for the two millions returned as being present at worship other than that of the Church, constitute almost the whole numerical strength of Dissent, certainly above two-thirds of that strength; whereas the 2,371,000 attending Church worship do not represent one-fourth, or anything like it, of those nominally belonging to the Church. This is, of course, not to the credit of the Church, but it is a fact which cannot be gainsayed. The sects, from the very circumcumstance of their being select bodies, not only exercise more effective discipline, which keeps up a certain religious standard within the limits of the sect; but from the fact of each member of them choosing, or being supposed to choose, his sect for himself, he naturally takes more interest in that which constitutes its distinctive character. There is, among the sects, far less of the hereditary, and far more of the free choice principle. The former is as much as possible ignored, and the latter encouraged. In addition to all this we have to remember to our shame that the sects represent the vigorous Methodistic revival of religion, while the Church was benumbed with the torpor of the eighteenth century. These things put together amply account for my assertion that the numbers given at the census of 1851, represent almost, if not altogether, the whole numerical strength of Dissent, and not a fifth, or perhaps, a sixth, of the nominal adherents of the Church.

After a careful consideration of all ascertainable facts bearing on this matter, I believe that the Church of England may be legitimately said to number 75 per cent of the population of England; and that of the remaining 25 per cent, not half, perhaps not a third, would reject her services and the ministrations of her clergy in the sense that the Romanists of Ireland reject the ministrations of the clergy of Ireland. The Irish Roman Catholic absolutely rejects the religious ministrations of the Irish Protestant clergyman. He may be on very friendly terms with him, he may entrust his money to his keeping, but he will not on any consideration receive any ordinance of religion from him. He will not suffer him to pray by his bedside, or to baptize his child; and he would have to do penance as for a mortal sin, if he ever attended worship in his church. A remarkable illustration of this occurred at the installation of the Prince of Wales as Knight of St. Patrick. The heads of the Roman Catholic Church in Dublin were appealed to as to whether it was lawful for Roman Catholics to attend St. Patrick's Cathedral on that occasion, and the answer given was, that they might, because it was not a religious service, but a state pageant. Such an occurrence is scarcely conceivable in this country.

The Dissenters of England in times of sickness, especially throughout the country districts, look for the ministrations of the clergy, and I have heard them complain with much bitterness, when owing to neglect or to any other cause, such ministrations have been withheld.

But this is by no means all which must be taken into account. Another very important consideration is, that the hold which the various religious bodies in England have on their adherents, and on the children of those adherents, is the loosest possible, whereas the hold of the Romish Church is the firmest. You can never tell from the profession of an English father, what is the profession of his grown up children. You cannot even tell from the profession of the father, to what Sunday School he sends his children.

A number of parishes may be cited where the Church seems at the lowest ebb : scarcely a handful attends her ministrations, but it is not for a moment to be supposed that the population is alienated from the Church in the sense in which the population of Ireland is alienated. I have known numbers of instances where the Church has been emptied by one minister and filled by his successor in a month or two. Two such instances have occurred within a few miles of where I now write.

I am well aware in writing this, of the vast seething heathenism in our metropolis and large towns; but it is to be remembered that these masses hold aloof from the Church, simply through irreligion, and it is within the power of self denial and labour to win them over: indeed their alienation is nothing to what it was at the time of the first reform bill. It was hostility then, it is apathy now. On the part of the English masses, it is irreligious alienation; on the part of the Irish it is religious. The people of Ireland hold aloof from the Church of Ireland from religious conviction, erroneous but determined; and are certainly more religious in their way, than the Irish Protestants are in theirs.

Another point of essential difference between England and Ireland is this, that whereas the dissidents from the Church of Ireland form one compact body, having one creed, one ritual, and one most perfect organization, the dissidents from the Church of England are in no such sense one.

One body, the Roman Catholic Church, represents the religious feeling of the population, whereas no one organization of English dissent can possibly compete with the Church of England as the expression of English national religious feeling.

There are historical and national considerations which will always weigh with educated Englishmen in favour of the English Church. Account for it as we may it is a most certain fact that, with very few exceptions, all English religious literature which lives is Church

of England. Still more is this true of secular literature : if any religious standpoint at all is taken in secular
literature, it is, as a rule, that of the Church. The
writers in newspapers, and notably those of most circu-
lation, always seem to take some Church ground, or if
not, some infidel ground ; no matter how they vilify
the clergy and patronize the Nonconformists they never
take Wesleyan or Congregational ground. If they
attack religion it is through the Church. If they
desire to fight out a principle they assume that it is to be
fought out within the Church. Considering the numbers,
wealth, and intelligence of Dissenters, I own I am sur-
prised how completely their distinctive principles are
ignored, but so it is.

Taking all this into account it is difficult to
estimate the secret hold the Church has on the
national mind and heart. It is hard to conceive the
Church brought lower than she was in the times of the
Rebellion and Protectorate. During that long disastrous
period her services were proscribed for above 20 years in
vast numbers of parishes, and for 15 years in all. Her
cause was associated with civil tyranny and oppression.
Moreover the forces arrayed against her acted with
ten-fold more religious energy then than now. The
strongest religious movement of this day cannot be named
beside the relentless Calvanistic fanaticism of the
Ironsides. The Church was then, to all human seeming,
as a national institution, extinct. A few educated
persons here and there met in secret to console themselves
with her services. And yet the moment a free parliament
was called the Church was restored on a higher basis than

ever, not by the will of the Monarch but by the will of the nation.

I am well aware of the seeming progress of notions, (they can hardly be called' principles) inimical to all establishment of religion. I, however, do not for a moment hesitate to affirm that the national mind of England has never attempted to realize the question of the severance of Church and State in England, and I . will give two or three reasons for this assertion.

First of all the example of America is cited, as if it makes against Church Establishments, that the American people, when they asserted their independence, did not establish any form of religion, whereas they could not have done so, simply because at the time of the War of Independence there was no sect of such preponderating influence that it could be assumed to represent the national religious expression of the community. If, any form of Christianity had been so proponderating, the state, as representing the lay element of the nation, must have entered into relations with the Church, whose organization, no matter what its tenets, is necessarily, in a great degree, clerical or sacerdotal. The state or lay element must have done so in self-defence, not for the purpose of enslaving the clerical element, but simply to make it keep its place and so preserve its religious life ; and what I ask, can these relations be but some form of establishment. If in any country any compact body of religionists act in concert and are so numerous as to sway the national representative councils, the state must have some permanent understanding with them i.e., must virtually establish them. If Ireland were to have her own parliament, and that parliament fairly representing her masses, it is clear that if, on the principles of the Liberation Society, the state were to take no cognizance of her religion, it would simply be making her over, bound hand and foot, into the power of an Italian bishop.

The principles of the Liberation Society are powerless in the face of such an organization as that of Rome. If the Roman Catholic Church is in a minority in any state, she will, of course, claim the benefit of them, as she does now in Ireland. Give her a self-governing majority and she would treat them as heresy.

Another pretty plain proof that the national mind has not for a moment faced the question of the disendowment of the Church of England is this, that it is no uncommon thing to hear of persons proposing to disestablish the Church in order to get rid of "Ritualism." Disestablishment is a rod perpetually held *in terrorem* over the Church, to make her do what the state has withheld from her all power of doing, *viz :*—of repressing extravagancies.

Consider for a moment the reasonableness of taking such a line.

In every country of Europe, with the single exception of the Roman states, the state more immediately represents the lay element of any Christian Kingdom, and the Church the clerical; so that for any state to take the " Liberation " ground is simply to leave the clerical or sacerdotal element as much as possible to itself. Now seeing that Ritualism (whether rightly or wrongly I do not say), is held to be an extreme development of

D

sacerdotalism, it seems on general or abstract grounds, a singular way of discouraging it to withdraw all state interference, and by so doing to leave the sacerdotal element in which it is supposed to flourish, more unfettered. But this singularity resolves itself into still grosser absurdity when we enter into particulars, for consider this for a moment. The places where Ritualism flourishes are in the Metropolis, and large towns, such as Brighton—notably in the Metropolis. Now in London, and in all our large towns, the Church as a whole, is to all intents and purposes disendowed. Whatever endowments it has are, as a rule, in no sense national, but are much the same as the endowments of the older meeting houses. Now the only rod that the state can hold over the Church is the loss of its national endowments, which endowments are very seldom indeed held by Ritualists, who in many cases avow themselves Liberationists; so that by taking this line you threaten certain country rectors, whose services in God's house (generally the minimum) are as bare as puritanism or neglect can make them, with the loss of their endowments (rather of the endowments of their successors) in order to bring to reason certain other clergy who never finger a penny of endowment, who depend upon the alms and freewill offerings of those who agree with them, and who would have no objection to see Church and State severed tomorrow. We used to hear of robbing Peter to pay Paul, this is like whipping Peter to make Paul feel. If the national mind then thinks to wash its hands of Ritualism by disestablishing its Church, it shews pretty plainly that it has never faced the question of the disestablishment of so exceedingly varied an institution as the Church of England.

I will give a third and last instance.

One of the arguments most frequently put forth by the opponents of the connection of Church and State is that the union intensifies sectarian animosities. Mr. Miall himself has, in a speech delivered not long ago, declared that if we could only destroy the connection between Church and State, religious animosities, if not religious differences, would disappear. Now this seems very odd, seeing that the lay mind (in the case of every religious organization) is supposed to be, and no doubt is, less sectarian than the clerical, and the connection between Church and State, in England at least, takes the form of the lay mind influencing or controlling the clerical, and certainly not in the direction of making it more sectarian.

But this very year has furnished us with two incidents which, taken together, surprisingly illustrate the real state of the case. Everybody must remember that a few months ago, the Dean of the Metropolitan Cathedral of England took prominent part in a festival of the Calvinistic Methodists : whether he assisted in the service in the chapel, I am unable to say, but in the after dinner speech, he certainly delivered himself in such terms as to leave the impression, that he thought the ministry of that body on the whole superior to his own, for it had at least contrived to keep itself from certain extravagancies, which have undoubtedly formed a lodgment in his (the Dean's) system.

Some months before this, a Mr. Tyng, an American clergyman, had taken a similar part in the services of the American Baptists, and it was at once felt to be a matter for the exercise of grave discipline. The matter was brought before the convention of the diocese—a lay as well as a clerical body, and that convention directed the Bishop as the servant of the Church to reprove the offending clergyman.

I need hardly say, that we read of no such reproof having been administered to the Dean, either by his Metropolitan, or by the Bishop of the diocese in which the College was situated, or by Convocation.

I do not for a moment pronounce on the merits of these two cases. It may be that, in the sight of God, the Church of the United States is called to bear more direct testimony among the Babel of sects there, to the claims of the Apostolic ministry. It may be also that in this country the Church should, in the sight of the same God, bear witness to the fact that whilst she has been asleep or lukewarm, the sects have been awake and energetic, and so have done some of the work her Master commissioned her to do.

I pronounce, as I said, no opinion on it at all. I merely draw attention to the fact that the Unestablished Church considered the ignoring of difference a matter of discipline, and that the Established Church did not.

The conclusions then to which I have been led are these.

The disestablishment of the Church of Ireland is a thing demanded by justice and common sense. It is impossible to uphold its continuance as a National

Church on any principles on which Church establishments can be upheld.   It is impossible to uphold it, on
the assumption that England and Ireland are one nation,
for they are not, and never will be as long as the Celtic
element prevails in Ireland.   The assumption that it is
a Missionary Church, seems fatal to its claims to be an
establishment.   The defence set up for it that it represents the original Church of St. Patrick, seems to me to
fail utterly.

But the circumstances under which Anglican Protestantism has existed, and yet exists, in Ireland, are
such as to render anything like the total disendowment
of the Irish Church as proposed by some, a monstrous
injustice.

It is a cruel wrong to cast a poor and scattered people
on the voluntary system, in circumstances most adverse
to the success of that system, and to take no material
guarantee from the landed proprietors, (most of them
absentees), that they will maintain among them the
rites of Protestant worship and the means of Protestant
instruction.   The Celtic population will not respect us
the more if, under pretence of dealing justly with
them, we deal hardly and cruelly with those who have
held, and perhaps yet hold, Ireland for us.

Let the Legislature then deal justly with the Irish
nation and with the Protestant "garrison."   Let the case
of each parish be considered on its own merits.

If the Parliament determines to take away the Ecclesiastical Revenues in parishes where there is little or no
work for the clergyman, let us console ourselves with
the thought that if the past century of our own

Church's history has taught us one lesson, it is this, that the most evil thing which the Church of Christ can endure within it, is a sinecure. Spoliation is, at the worst, but the blow from without, bruising the surface, the sinecure is the cancer poisoning the life blood.

If the British Parliament in the exercise of that " Omnipotence " which can seize the property of any Church, sect, connection, or society, proposes utterly to despoil the Church, let it remember that the whole issue is in the hands of One Who can disestablish and disendow States as well as Churches.

When its members propose to throw a Church long endowed like that of Ireland, on alms and subscriptions for its maintenance, just as other bodies of dissenters are, on the pretence that religion will flourish more if disendowed; let them bear in mind, that God has pronounced far more clearly on the deadening effects of riches on " persons," than on Churches, and if, for mere party convenience, they think to cast the Church of Ireland on the world to purify it, God may take them at their word—apply the same rule to them, and make their souls to prosper at the cost of their possessions.

All is in His hands, but if in His hands, then see we to it that we fully recognize such a fact.

We are told on one side that no matter how just and needful disestablishment is, still that the exigencies of party require that we should uphold the wrong in order to save the right.

We are told on the other side that it is too late for a reformed Parliament to temper justice with mercy.

I trust that we ministers of Christ have not so learned Christ, as to imagine that He allows His Church to depend, even for its worldly maintenance, on the results of party tactics.

We have to discern and choose the right—like the Prophet-Priest of Old, we have to "take forth the precious from the vile," to disentangle right from wrong, and at any cost to uphold what is right and to reject what is wrong.

That in this matter we may all be guided so to do, is

My Reverend Brethren,

The desire and hope of

Your obedient humble Servant,

M. F. SADLER.

JAMES R. PORTER, PRINTER, HIGH STREET, BEDFORD.

WORKS BY THE SAME AUTHOR.

CHURCH DOCTRINE—BIBLE TRUTH. Third Edition. 5s.

Opinions of the Press.

Mr. Sadler takes Church Doctrine, specifically so called, subject by subject, and elaborately shows its specially marked Scripturalness. The objective nature of the faith, the Athanasian Creed, the Baptismal Services, the Holy Eucharist, Absolution and the Priesthood, Church Government and Confirmation, are some of the more prominent subjects treated. And Mr. Sadler handles each with a marked degree of sound sense, and with a thorough mastery of his subject."—*The Guardian, April 26th,* 1865.

" We know of no recent work, professing to cover the same ground, in which the agreement of our Church Services with the Scripture, is more amply vindicated."—From an adverse review in *Christian Observer, October,* 1866.

EMMANUEL: or, the Incarnation of the Son of God, the Foundation of Immutable Truth. 10s. 6d.

Opinions of the Press.

"Where Mr. Sadler is eminently successful is in shewing how the great Catholic doctrine is vitally and inseparably connected with the New Testament; and further, on what shallow views, at once of the doctrine itself, and of the realities of the world, and of human nature, the general objections of Rationalism are based; how idle and childish it is to admit a Revelation, with the Incarnation and Resurrection, and yet on any general grounds to make objection to the details of a miraculous dispensation."—*Guardian, Jan.* 16th, 1867.

" His argument is constructed on the inductive method, and hence he first lays his foundations, broad and deep, by exhibiting the teachings of the New Testament on the doctrine of our Lord's person; taking the different writers separately, pointing out with great care how much each contribute to the elucidation of the truth, and indicating the agreement of their several testimonies. His examination is very careful and instructive, marked by considerable exegetical skill, and full of suggestions of the highest value to the Biblical student."—*Christian World, April 12th,* 1868.

PARISH SERMONS. Vols. I. and II. Second Edition. 6s.

THE SECOND ADAM AND THE NEW BIRTH. 4s. 6d.

THE SACRAMENT OF RESPONSIBILITY. Sixpence.

A library edition of the latter in preparation.

London: Bell and Daldy. Bedford: James R. Porter.

www.ingramcontent.com/pod-product-compliance
Lightning Source LLC
Chambersburg PA
CBHW031758090426
42739CB00008B/1072